GUARDING AREA 51

BY BRANDON TERRELL

The Child's World®
childsworld.com

Published by The Child's World®
1980 Lookout Drive • Mankato, MN 56003-1705
800-599-READ • www.childsworld.com

Acknowledgments
The Child's World®: Mary Swensen, Publishing Director
Red Line Editorial: Editorial direction and production
The Design Lab: Design

Design Element: Iaroslav Neliubov/Shutterstock Images
Photographs ©: Jon Elswick/AP Images, cover, 1; Stocktrek Images/Corbis, 5; Petty Officer 3rd Class Patrick Kelley/U.S. Coast Guard, 6; Public Domain, 7; AP Images, 9, 10; HO/AP Images, 12; CIA, 16; Laura Rauch/AP Image, 18; NASA, 20

ISBN 9781503808096
LCCN 2015958274

Printed in the United States of America
PA02349

ABOUT THE AUTHOR

Brandon Terrell is a Saint Paul-based writer of numerous children's books, including picture books, chapter books, and graphic novels. When not hunched over his laptop, Brandon enjoys watching movies and television, reading, playing baseball, and spending every spare moment with his wife and their two children.

TABLE OF CONTENTS

CHAPTER 1

Restricted Area

In the heart of the Nevada desert is a secret military base. For a long time almost nobody spoke much about it. The base is still difficult to enter even though it is **declassified**. The base is located approximately 75 miles (121 km) outside of Las Vegas. It was built around a dry lake bed called Groom Lake. That was more than 60 years ago. The site is inside the boundaries of the Nellis Air Force Range. That is a military training area.

The name of this mysterious site is called Area 51. Whenever Area 51 was mentioned in government documents, its name was blocked out with black ink.

Area 51 has sparked imaginations for years. Many believe alien bodies are there. Some think there might be unidentified flying objects (UFOs), too. These theories grew over decades. For a while the government never said whether Area 51 even existed.

Nellis Air Force Base in Nevada is a training venue for the U.S. Air Force.

That changed in 2013. President Barack Obama declassified part of a large document. It was about the site. It was the first time the government admitted the site existed. The thick document did not mention aliens or UFOs. It focused on two of the site's **reconnaissance** airplane programs: the U-2 and the A-12 OXCART.

So how does one get into Area 51? It is not easy.

There is a restricted area. Visitors need top secret security clearance to enter. But that's not all. They also need an invitation. These come from the U.S. military or other intelligence agencies. Visitors are sworn to secrecy. They take an oath to not talk about

President Barack Obama shone some light on the previously secret location known as Area 51 in 2013.

what they see. Those who break it could be thrown in jail.

It is the same for those working at the facility. Buildings at Area 51 have no windows. This keeps employees from getting distracted. It also means workers do not know what projects their coworkers are doing. Supervisors also keep this information secret.

It is difficult to see the base from far away. But that might be the best chance to get a glimpse. The government bought land around the area. This stops hikers from seeing what is happening. There is a way for outsiders to see Area 51 from the

A view from Tikaboo Peak, about 26 miles away from Area 51.

ground. It involves a hard hike up Tikaboo Peak. The mountain is 26 miles (42 km) from the base. Flashing lights from one of Area 51's runways can occasionally be seen. Rarely, an airplane takes off or lands.

Not much else is known about Area 51. Security and secrecy keep what happens inside a mystery to most.

NAMING THE SITE

There are still many mysteries surrounding Area 51. One is the history of the site's name. Nobody is sure just how Area 51 got its title. Many think it has to do with a mapping system, though. They think the land was broken up into numbered sections around the time the site was created.

CHAPTER 2

The Early Days

It was 1955. The Central Intelligence Agency (CIA) needed a secret facility. They had to test an aircraft. It was needed to watch over the Soviet Union. The Soviets had a dangerous nuclear weapons program.

Top CIA officials flew across the Mojave Desert. The desert stretches from California to Nevada. They found Groom Lake. It was a test site. The government's **atomic** bomb program was there. The area was already secret.

The hard ground at Groom Lake was perfect. It even had a small runway. It was most likely built during World War II for training pilots to make emergency landings. The land and airstrip would do the job. They were added to the neighboring Atomic Energy Commission's Nevada Test Site.

The entire area was named Area 51.

Dr. J. Robert Oppenheimer was one of the leaders of the atomic bomb program.

At first, the military base was just a series of tents and an airplane hangar. Workers wore heavy boots to avoid rattlesnake bites. When the sun set each day, the entire area was pitch black.

U-2 spy planes, like the one shown here in 1957, did not fly fast but could stay in the air for long stretches of time.

It seemed like nothing more than a vast sea of sand. But there was more going on. Top-secret airplanes were being built.

The Cold War was happening at the time. It was between the United States and the Soviet Union. The Soviet Union is now known as Russia. There were not any direct battles between the two countries. But both were worried about each other's weapons. The United States wanted to keep its weapons secret. The U.S. Air Force, the CIA, and the National Aeronautics and Space Administration (NASA) were working on **supersonic** and **stealth** technology. This was why Area 51 remained a secret.

Workers at the Groom Lake site did not always call it Area 51. Sometimes they called it Paradise Ranch or just the Ranch.

The first CIA spy plane built and tested at Area 51 was the U-2. The program was named Project OARFISH.

The planes were shipped in pieces to Area 51. Workers there put them together. The U-2 had a thin aluminum outside. It also had a pointy **fuselage**. Its wings were long and sleek. They sagged at the end and almost touched the ground. This was a problem. Mechanics often ran alongside the plane during takeoff. They held up the wings so they would not scrape the ground. The plane was very fragile. That made it hard to fly.

SR-71 Blackbird planes were out of service for six years due to high costs before returning in 1995.

The U-2 spy plane could fly at 70,000 feet (21,336 m). It gathered **surveillance**. It could glide overhead for hours.

The U-2 is still used today. It is still fragile. But it is 40 percent larger now. It has a digital instrument panel. Its engine is more efficient.

DREAMLAND

Area 51 has several nicknames. One is Dreamland. The name supposedly comes from the title of a poem by Edgar Allan Poe. He is a famous writer. Two of his most famous works are "The Raven" and "The Tell-Tale Heart." A line from "Dreamland" reads: "But the traveler, traveling through it / May not—dare not openly view it / Never its mysteries are exposed / To the weak human eye unclosed. . ."

Area 51 was cleared out in 1957. Nuclear tests were being conducted 11 miles (17.7 km) away in Los Alamos, New Mexico. A nuclear bomb was detonated. A mushroom cloud blocked out the sky. Reports said its **fallout** would contaminate the Groom Lake facility. So the facility was evacuated.

The CIA had a new mission in September 1959. The U-2 spy planes were a success. But they needed camouflage. A new project, Project OXCART, began at Area 51. The new airplane was different from the U-2. It could fly at 90,000 feet (27,432 m). It was five times faster than the U-2. The OXCART plane reached 2,200 mph (3,540 kmh). It could also beat Soviet radars.

The new spy plane became known as the Archangel-12. It was called A-12 for short.

EXPANSION

Project OXCART was enormous. So Area 51 had to expand. A new, 8,500-foot (2,590 m) long runway was built. It was put together at night. This helped keep it more secret. The A-12 needed almost 186 miles (299 km) to make a U-turn. So the airspace around the base needed to be widened. An extra 38,400 acres (15,540 h) of public land was added to Area 51 in 1938.

Other well-known planes were created and tested at Area 51. One was the SR-71 Blackbird. The F-117 Nighthawk stealth fighter and the B-2 stealth bomber were also born there. These airplanes reached up to Mach 3. That is three times the speed of sound. The speed of sound is 761 mph (1,225 kmh).

People watching the sky above Area 51 saw lights streaking overhead. Such sights have made Area 51 mysterious over the years.

CHAPTER 3

Classified

The existence of Area 51 has been declassified. But the details of the facility are still a mystery. Some information has been verified. But much more has not. The government has made it difficult to know exactly what is going on inside. Mapmakers have been told to leave out the buildings and the road leading to Area 51.

The site is considered an official Military Operating Area. There are no protective fences surrounding it. Signs and orange poles are posted around the borders. The signs warn that trespassers will be fined. The signs say security can use deadly force if necessary.

Guards in camouflage patrol the borders. They work in pairs. Sensors are buried around the perimeter. They detect the slightest movement.

More runways and buildings have been added since the 1960s. Airspace above Area 51 is

MAPPING OUT AREA 51

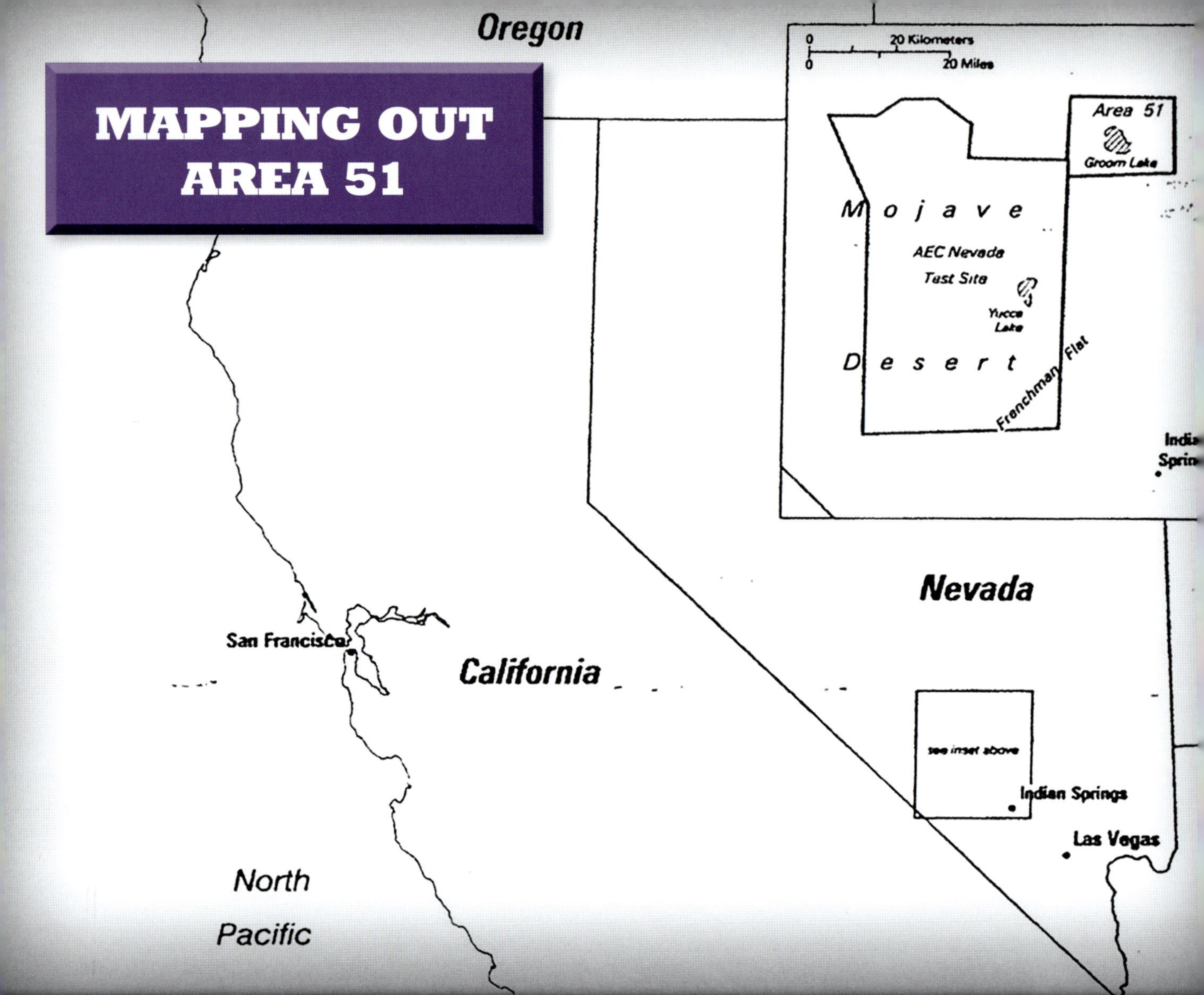

restricted. This keeps anybody from looking down at Area 51. Satellites orbiting Earth are an exception. The only planes allowed onto the base are unmarked. They use the call sign "Janet" followed by three digits.

Knowing what Area 51 looks like from the outside is difficult. Learning what is hidden inside is even harder. Everything that happens at the facility is top secret. It is all on a need-to-know basis.

Very few people need to know. But here is what is known.

Area 51 is comprised of 90,000 acres (36,422 ha) of land. The main base, including buildings and runways, makes up a small percentage of this land. There is a hangar near a guard shack. There is also some housing there.

There is a mess hall where workers eat. There are shelters known as "hide and scoots." They are called this because they offer cover for airplanes and **personnel** when a satellite or unauthorized plane flies overhead.

But what is inside the hangar? And how deep does it go? Some say the facility is mainly located underground. They believe there are 40 levels of maze-like tunnels in the base. There are other rumors, too. They say there are underground rail

The government of Nevada established the Extraterrestrial Highway, which runs along the eastern border of Area 51, in 1996.

systems. These people believe the systems connect Area 51 to sites along the West Coast. These places include Los Alamos and Los Angeles. But this is highly unlikely. It would be too hard to complete such a large job.

The fact these rumors exist says a lot. When it comes to what is hiding within and under the walls of Area 51, the public is in the dark.

RICHARD MINGUS

Richard Mingus was one of the first Area 51 security guards. He watched over the facility during the nearby nuclear tests in 1957. He manned the gate after the explosion of one of the largest atomic bombs in U.S. history. He was also in charge of the only Area 51 phone to receive calls. He did not confirm nor deny workers' names when answering. He also did not share his location.

CHAPTER 4

Access Denied

There is another major part of the Area 51 mysteries. It involves discussion of UFOs. The base is linked to alien **conspiracy** theories.

An aircraft crashed in the desert near Roswell, New Mexico, in July 1947. A rancher discovered the wreckage. He found metal debris and foil reflectors in his sheep pasture. He called the sheriff, who contacted the U.S. Air Force. The Air Force took away the debris.

The Air Force called the craft a weather balloon. They closed the matter. Members of the public were not pleased. They thought the debris was part of an alien spaceship.

Robert Lazar used to work at Area 51. He went on TV in 1989. Lazar said he was part of a group that studied alien technology. He said he saw nine spaceships in a part of Area 51. It was known as S-4. He also said he saw small gray aliens with

Some people believe one of the most famous moments in American history was staged at Area 51.

large heads. Lazar's claims were investigated. Some were declared false. Lazar took lie detector tests. They did not provide a firm answer.

The theories about aliens and UFOs are just the beginning. There are plenty of other wild rumors about what is happening at Area 51.

Some believe there is a secret organization called Majestic. It is also called Majic 12. People say it has 12 of the most powerful men and women in the country. It includes former presidents. People say the Majic 12 uses alien technology from Area 51. Their supposed goal is to try to take over the world.

UFO believers also talk about Hangar 18. It is said to be the building where aliens and their ships are studied. Many think Hangar 18 is located at Area 51.

MAN ON THE MOON

July 20, 1969, is one of the most famous days in U.S. history. Neil Armstrong and Buzz Aldrin were part of the Apollo 11 mission. That day, they became the first two men to walk on the moon. However, some are not so sure it ever happened. Some people doubt the footage captured by the Apollo 11 mission. They believe the whole thing was filmed at Area 51.

Not all theories are about aliens. Some involve spy planes. One is the Aurora. It is supposedly an airplane capable of traveling more than Mach 5. Another plane is the Mothership. Theorists say it is a large jet. The jet allows a smaller airplane to launch from it in midair.

Officially, the name Area 51 has not been a secret since 2013. But what happens at the facility certainly still is.

GLOSSARY

atomic (uh-TAHM-ik) Something is atomic when it is related to tiny particles called atoms. Atomic bombs have been tested in the area around Area 51.

conspiracy (kuhn-SPIR-uh-see) A conspiracy is a secret plot to do something wrong or against the law. There are many conspiracy theories about what takes place at Area 51.

declassified (dee-KLAS-uh-fyed) Declassified materials are things that were once kept secret but have been made open to the public. In 2013, the U.S. government declassified documents that mentioned the existence of Area 51.

fallout (FALL-out) Fallout is the material that falls to the ground after an explosion. The fallout from the detonation of a huge atomic bomb forced the closure of Area 51.

fuselage (FYOO-suh-lahzh) The fuselage is the main part or body of an airplane. The U-2 plane had a pointed fuselage.

personnel (per-suh-NEL) Personnel are people employed by a business or organization. The personnel of Area 51 take cover in "hide and scoot" shelters when unidentified vehicles fly overhead.

reconnaissance (ri-KAHN-uh-suntz) Reconnaissance is the act of searching for useful military information. Reconnaissance planes have been built and tested at Area 51.

stealth (STELTH) Something is stealth if it is secret or hard to detect. Stealth planes are important for countries in wartime.

supersonic (soo-pur-SAHN-ik) A supersonic vehicle can travel faster than the speed of sound. The United States was working on supersonic technology at Area 51 during the Cold War.

surveillance (sur-VAY-luntz) Surveillance is the act of watching closely. U-2 spy planes are used to gather surveillance.

TO LEARN MORE

IN THE LIBRARY

Haney, Jill. *Area 51*. Guangzhou, China: Saddleback Educational Publishing, 2015.

Karst, Ken. *Area 51*. Mankato, MN: Creative Company, 2015.

Zimmerman, Dwight Jon. *Area 51: The Graphic History of America's Most Secret Military Installation*. Minneapolis, MN: Zenith Press, 2014.

ON THE WEB

Visit our Web site for links about guarding Area 51: **childsworld.com/links**

Note to Parents, Teachers, and Librarians: We routinely verify our Web links to make sure they are safe and active sites. So encourage your readers to check them out!

INDEX